BECAUSE OF YOU

A Memoir of Growing, Grieving & Mothering without a Mother

Leigh Vozzella

To the three most important women in my life— my mother, Coral, for inadvertently making me the woman I am today, my grandmother, Irene, for leading me through life with guidance, kindness and wisdom and my daughter, Gianna, for showing me the meaning of the true love between a mother and daughter.

Your journey has molded you for your greater good, and it was exactly what it needed to be. Don't think that you've lost time. It took each and every situation you have encountered to bring you to the now. And now is right on time.

—Asha Tyson

INTRODUCTION

The book that you hold in your hands is not the book I originally intended to write. When I embarked on this journey I didn't intend to write a book at all, just a way of documenting and working through my own inner emotions after my mother's diagnosis of H.I.V.

Eighteen years ago when I began writing the words and pages which have become this book, my life was very different; I was very different. Back then I was a head-strong seventeen year old who lacked self-worth and self-confidence, despite putting on a good show. I was a people pleaser, a "yes-ma'am" if you will. I never rocked the boat, always did what was expected of me and desperately just wanted my mother's love and approval.

I never thought that I would ever turn my very personal thoughts, experiences and feelings into something for others to read. Hell, I rarely share my inner-most thoughts and feelings with those closest to me, let alone a bunch of strangers! And yet, that's what I have done; that is where this journey of growing and grieving over the last eighteen years has taken me.

Filled with divorce, homelessness, domestic violence, physical, mental, verbal and sexual abuse, poverty, terminal illness and drug addiction, my childhood was anything but easy, and my relationship with my mother was pretty non-existent at best.

After graduating high school at 16 and living on my own pretty much since then, having been kicked out of the house permanently at 17-years-old, I did what most young women do— I met a guy. Nick and I were a train wreck waiting to happen from the very start, but it was one filled with an abundance of life experience. An unplanned pregnancy very early on in our relationship resulted in not only our first son, but also in a marriage out of obligation rather than love. Four children, 14 and one half years later, with nearly 12 of them spent as husband and wife, and that train wreck became a natural disaster called divorce.

As much as this book is a memoir of my entire life, I really began writing it as a way to process my warped relationship with my mother. Through my childhood traumas, being kicked out of the house and pretty much banished from her life and home at the age of 17, reconnecting with her after she found out that she was H.I.V positive, becoming a mother for the first time and then losing her just as we began to have a "normal" mother-daughter relationship; writing this book has been part of the healing process for me. The driving force behind turning this document that I had been adding to for years into the book you hold today was the birth of my third child, my daughter Gianna.

For many women, our relationships with our mothers and with our daughters are at the core of our emotional lives. Our experiences as mothers *and* daughters shape our ideas, conversations, and interactions in all other relationships in our lives. While I didn't have a relationship with my mother to fall back on in my own mothering, I did have my grandmother, Irene, who has always been my strongest ally and my biggest supporter. Having two sons was one thing, but having a daughter scared the hell out of me; the only thing I knew of the mother-daughter relationship was what I personally experienced growing up. Not only was I hell bent on breaking the cycle of abuse in general as I mothered my own children, but I have always paid extra close attention to the relationship between my daughter and I, for I know that this is one of the most important relationships to her emotional and psychological development.

As a survivor of abuse, both physical and emotional at the hands of my mother and then sexual abuse at the hands of a close male friend of hers, my experiences have certainly shaped not only the person, but the mother I have become. No one is perfect and I'm not saying that I'm Super Mom, nor am I trying to be, but my own experiences keep me conscience of what to do, and not to do, with my own children.

Regardless of my strained relationship with my mother, being a motherless mother, well, it sucks to be quite honest. As daughters, no matter the relationship we have with our mothers, we still need them in our lives. As abusive and volatile as my relationship was with my mother and me, I still needed her and wanted her when I was pregnant with my first child. I still craved her life experience when I was pregnant with my second child and especially when I was going through my divorce.

Wounds heal, scars fade, but the emotional wreckage and baggage left behind after the death of a parent, especially when that parent-child relationship was turbulent, it can be more painful and traumatic than the actual relationship itself. I've spent years riddled with anger, guilt, depression, rage, and grief over the loss of my mother. It is certainly a void that never really gets filled, and leaves you, the motherless daughter, trying to navigate being a woman, a daughter, a mother without a mother.

Writing the words that became the pages of this book was a journey for me; a journey of self-discovery, of grieving and of healing. If you are struggling with an estranged mother-daughter relationship, if your mother died while you were young or after you were grown, the emptiness is still similar no matter how the exact circumstances differ. We are all daughters without mothers, trying to navigate womanhood, and maybe motherhood, without a compass.

If you are one of these motherless daughters as I am, I truly hope that in reading my words you find what will heal you, be it a friend who understands your trauma, some direction in the healing process, or simply just to know that you are not alone in this journey.

Healing doesn't mean that the damage never existed, it means that it no longer controls our lives— Unknown

Leigh Vozzella
June 2014

"For some moments in life, there are no words." ~David Seltzer, Willy Wonka and the Chocolate Factory

There are certain major events in our lives that we remember every detail of. Most people who were alive when JFK was assassinated remember exactly where they were when they heard the news. Mention 9/11 and just about everyone can tell you exactly what they were doing, who they were with, etc. The birth of a child, a marriage, a death; certain events etch themselves into our memories forever, some more so than others. I will never forget the phone call I received on the afternoon of November 11, 1998.

I was playing with my oldest son, 14 months old, when the phone rang; my mother's breathless voice was on the other end of the line. "I'm at Albany Med. and I'm not gonna make it home," she softly and slowly told me between gasps of breath. "What do you mean? What are you talking about Ma?" Choking back tears, she continued, "I know this is a sucky time for this to happen and I love you", "Ma stop it! What are you talking about?!" "I'm sick and I'm not going to make it home. I love you." "OK I'm coming up there; I'm leaving now, OK? I'll be there soon." "OK, bring the baby. I love you" My mother was not expressive when it came to emotions so, the simple fact that she just told me she loved me three times in the same phone call really drove home what she was trying to tell me. The inevitable day we had all been dreading for the past two years had arrived. I grabbed my purse, the diaper bag, car keys and my son and headed for the door.

My fiancé, Nick, and his parents tried, unsuccessfully, to stop me as I kept screaming, "my mother is dying! She's in the hospital and I need to leave NOW!" His mother tried to convince me to leave our son there with her, but I refused. My son meant everything to my mother and she specifically asked me to bring him, so I was going to do as she requested. I remember frantically looking for clothes and extra diapers, grabbing bottles and tossing things into a bag while Nick and his parents kept trying to calm me down and get me to slow down. "There's no time! I'm leaving NOW!" is all I kept saying to them. In my whirlwind of emotions, I called my grandmother and told her if she wanted to come she needed to be outside waiting for me in less than 10 minutes. I told Nick "you either need to get in the car or get out of my fucking way now!" Frightened of what might become of him if he continued to try and slow me down, he chose to get in the car. We picked my grandmother up and made what typically is a 3 ½ hour drive in less than 3 hours. 2 hours and 45 minutes to be exact.

We arrived at the Albany Medical Center parking garage at 9:03 pm. I had no idea where we needed to be; I hadn't taken the time to ask my mother what room or even what wing she was in. We quickly made our way inside and, with the help of a very patient nurse; we found my mother's room. Her breathing was labored and, despite her weak attempts at arguing to the contrary, she required constant oxygen.

She looked so small and frail lying there in that hospital bed. I put my son next to her and she immediately lit up. "Hey, my little buddy! Here's Grandma's boy! Come see Grandma." He crawled up and kissed her. We sat for a couple of minutes as she struggled to explain that she went to a routine doctor appointment that day, felt horrible and was sent to the hospital for more tests. The hospital admitted her and she rapidly declined over the past few hours. She began coughing, which turned into choking and saying, "it hurts! It hurts!" She then began having a seizure, which wasn't uncommon for her over the past several months. It felt as if time was standing still and everything was moving in slow motion. I remember doctors and nurses rushing into the room, yelling at me to get the baby out of the room. A nurse ushered us all to a family waiting area. As she spoke to us, all I could hear were muffled words. To me, she sounded like the teacher in all of the Peanuts episodes, her words sounding more like foreign noises than comprehensible words. I couldn't sit out there and wait, I ran back in. The doctors tried to stop the seizure and were attempting CPR. I remember calling my younger sister, who had just turned seventeen a few months earlier, and telling her to hurry. I was listed as my mother's health care proxy and she had a do not resuscitate order. The nurse behind the desk seemed as frantic as I was as she looked through my mother's medical record. I heard the words, "She has a DNR and I'm her proxy," come out of my mouth. I heard the nurse ask me what I wanted them to do and the only thing I could say to her was to repeat, "She has a DNR and I'm her proxy". The nurse put her hands on my shoulders and looked me in the eyes as she asked me again, "What would you like us to do?" "Nothing," I answered.

My mother passed away at 9:28 pm on Wednesday November 11, 1998, just one month and three days after her 39th birthday. The official cause was pulmonary arrest; the unofficial cause was H.I.V related complications.

That night was the longest night of my young life. My sister and her boyfriend came running down the hallway towards me just six minutes after the doctors called time of death. All I could say to her was, "It's too late." She began screaming, "No! No!" and hysterically sobbing as she punched and kicked the walls in the hallway where we stood. She went in and sat with our mother, holding her, telling her she loved her and sobbing uncontrollably. Nick, our son, my grandmother, my sister, her boyfriend and I all sat in the family room for what seemed like an eternity; in reality it was more like an hour. I went into my mother's hospital room and gathered up her belongings, signed the necessary paper work and got everyone moving towards the door so we could go home to my mother's house.

My mother still had a room set up for my son from when we lived there with her when he was an infant. I placed my sleeping child in his bed and tucked him into his Winnie the Pooh bedding; the blue light from the ten gallon fish tank, which my mother set up for him when he was a newborn, illuminated the room. The rest of us were emotionally drained, but mentally not ready for sleep. We sat around my mother's light maple kitchen table with the mismatched chairs that she attempted to recover with Contact paper repeatedly over the years. We eventually determined the sleeping arrangements: My grandmother would take my sister's room because it was the closest to the bathroom, Nick and I would take the pull out couch in the living room because it was closest to our son and my sister would take my old room upstairs. Everyone went off to their separate sleeping quarters for what was sure to be a sleepless night for all.

At some point I know that I dozed off ever so briefly; something made me jump from my sleep. The sofa bed that my fiancé and I were sleeping on faced our son's room which was really intended to be used as a den or study, I imagine, because it was open to the living room as opposed to having a wall separating the two spaces. When I jolted from my sleep this particular time, I vividly remember raising my head from the pillow, sitting upright and looking directly at my son's bedroom. As clear as day, as real as the heart beating within my chest, I saw my mother sitting on the edge of my son's bed, rubbing his back the way she did when he was an infant. I rubbed my eyes and blinked a few times. Surely I must be dreaming! No amount of blinking or rubbing made this image go away. Softly I said, "Ma, what are you doing here?" She put her finger to her pale pursed lips and said, "Shh, go back to sleep." And so I did.

Now, I must confess, I am by no means a religious person. My mother was a lapsed Catholic who knew that she believed in God and Jesus Christ, but wasn't so sure she believed in much of the Catholic teachings. When my sister and I were infants, she had us baptized, and we very briefly attended CCD classes for half of one school year. My mother was more of the "go, see, learn, explore" persuasion when it came to exposing my sister and I to any sort of religion. We attended Protestant Sunday school with friends of ours and learned about the Jewish faith from our uncle's long-time girlfriend. The summer between 8th and 9th grade, I became intrigued, and somewhat active, with the Seventh - day Adventist church that a good friend of mine belonged to.

Over the years I have thoroughly enjoyed learning about various religions, but have not found any that feel like the right "fit" for me. My reason behind explaining this is this— I have no idea what happens to our souls after we die, if anything, and I'm not going to debate whether there is an afterlife or not. However, I know what I saw that night when I looked into my son's bedroom and I am 100% without a doubt certain that my mother, in some form, was in fact sitting on my son's bed the night that she died, rubbing his back as he slept and telling me to go to sleep.

The next morning, after I made sure everyone had breakfast, it was time to get down to business. My sister and grandmother were still an utter emotional mess so I put them in charge of keeping my son busy. My first phone call of the day was to my best friend of seven years, the person who sometimes knew me better than I knew myself and the one person who I knew I could always count on. "Hi! What's up?" she answered in a tone that was way too cheery for me at that point. "Um… Danielle… I'm in New York." I could feel my temperature rise and my face flush as the burning tears welled up in my eyes, and she could tell something was wrong. Filled with concern, she began bombarding me with questions "What's wrong? What happened? Is everything OK? Are you OK?" "Um…no, not really," I answered, my voice trembling, as my eyes welled up with tears. "Tell me what's wrong, what happened?!" I could hear the feeling of helplessness in her voice. "Danielle, she died," was all I could muster. She immediately knew I meant my mother and said, "I'm on my way." Now, remember, this was 1998 which means pre-GPS. She had no idea how to get to my mother's house, but 4 hours later there she was at the back door hugging me and ready to jump in with whatever I needed from her at that point.

In the four hours that lapsed between my phone call to Danielle and her arrival, I had made the necessary phone calls to the funeral home my mother selected, made travel arrangements to have her body flown back to Massachusetts from New York, contacted local friends with details of a memorial service to be held at my mother's home, made the necessary phone calls to friends and family in Massachusetts, contacted the local New York newspaper with her obituary and selected clothing to give to the funeral director. All day long neighbors and friends were stopping by with food to express their condolences and each time I thought to myself, "Oh great! Another person to console! Don't these people understand I have a shit load of stuff to accomplish here?!" Don't get me wrong, I fully understand and appreciate that this is customary when someone dies, but in the moment I was completely annoyed by the whole process. After all, I not only needed to deal with visitors and play hostess to these people who were disrupting my lengthy to-do list, but I also had to put all of the food away and try to remember which dishes belonged to which friends so that they could later be returned to their rightful owner. In my inner tantrum of annoyance, I remember thinking, "Jesus! Haven't these people ever heard of disposable storage containers?"

I spent nearly two weeks holding everyone else together while I planned and arranged every detail per my mother's written request. I was nineteen at the time and a first-time mother myself, my son just fourteen months old. According to my mother's will, I was also now the guardian of my seventeen year old sister. I cooked, cleaned, planned and called.

Aside from my phone call to Danielle, not once since leaving the hospital did I shed a single tear. I didn't have time for the emotional breakdown I deserved because I was too busy taking care of everyone and everything else. I had spent the last couple of weeks doing exactly what was expected of me. I had spent my entire life hearing myself described by family members as the strong, responsible, organized one and I was certainly living up to it.

The loss of my mother didn't truly become a reality for me until the night of her wake. When I walked into the funeral home, a gorgeous and grand white building with forest green shutters and resembled a Southern plantation with its large white pillars and wrap around porch, the funeral director lead me to a room I knew too well. I felt my heart stop for a moment when I saw my mother lying in the exact same spot of the exact same room that my step-father, my sister's father, had been in just 10 ½ years earlier. The room, with its walls covered in Victorian-era style, rose-colored wallpaper on top and white wainscot below, looked exactly the same as it had all those years ago. The same perfectly polished hardwood floors protected with the same oriental runners; the windows neatly dressed in gorgeous dusty mauve and sage green draperies with deep gold tasseled trim along the valances. The room even smelled exactly as it did then—a mixture of warm vanilla sugar incense and fresh flowers.

I remember thinking that the florist did a beautiful job with the arrangements I ordered: a bouquet of red, pink, yellow, white and peach roses with a white silk ribbon reading "daughter", a cascade of pale lavender sterling roses with a purple ribbon that read "Ma" and a small, white silk pillow with a purple sash that read "Grandma". These three arrangements expressed a piece of who my mother was: a daughter, mother and grandmother who loved roses and the color purple. While we awaited the arrival of friends and family who would soon be there to pay their respect, I kept myself busy by displaying the individual photos around the room that I brought. As friends and family members took turns going up to her casket and paying their final respects, they each stopped at the head of my mother's casket to reminisce over the photo collage displaying various stages of my mother's life, each making a point to impress their memories of our mother's younger years upon my sister and I.

Surrounded by family and friends, my sister and I tried to contain our hysterical laughter at the irony of our somewhat racist, lapsed Catholic mother having a black Catholic priest, who spoke with a thick African accent, eulogize her. We couldn't help but think that at any second she was going to pop up and start screaming profanities at us for allowing such an event to take place. Of course, that didn't happen and the reality that it would never happen again slowly began to creep over us as our muffled laughter slowly transformed into hushed sobs. As every person in attendance hugged my sister and me, each expressing their deepest sympathies, it hit me. I had to get up, say goodbye to my mother and walk away from her for the very last time in my life. As the room emptied of our loved ones, I sat paralyzed in my seat at the mere thought of what I now had to find the strength to do.

With the help of Nick and Danielle, I mustered up whatever strength I had left, stood up, took a deep breath and slowly made my way to the casket where my mother laid in the clothes I had chosen for her, her favorite blush pink sweater dress. To think, just a week earlier I had been standing in my mother's bedroom trying to choose the perfect outfit and figuring out whether her apparel needed to include undergarments. I remember scrutinizing her face, half criticizing the make-up job and partly trying to burn the image of her face into my memory forever.

As I leaned down to kiss her goodbye, that's when it hit me. As my warm, fleshy lips touched her cold, rigid skin the realization that my mother was gone forever washed over me like a tsunami and I fell apart. I began hysterically sobbing and shouting, "She's so cold! I can't do this, she's just so cold!" I remember not being able to feel my feet on the floor, despite the fact that they were still firmly planted below me. My legs felt as if they were made out of Jell-O and I could feel myself falling to the floor. I remember the expressions of shock and helplessness on the faces of Nick and Danielle as they each stood there, arms outstretched, holding me up and attempting to hold me together. Neither of them had ever seen me lose my composure and certainly not to the point of hysteria and hyperventilation.

I eventually regained enough of my strength and composure to walk out of the funeral home and get in the car, but that night was the second longest night of my life. The ten minute car ride home seemed like an eternity and sleep was not in the cards either. No matter how exhausted my body felt, I could not stop the thoughts and mental images of my mother from stirring in my aching head. My entire childhood, every memory—good and bad, they all seemed to come rushing to the forefront of my subconscious that night. I relived every harsh word either of us had ever spoken, every opportunity I missed to spend time with her or tell her I loved her and appreciated her. They say guilt is part of the grieving process, but I never knew that it would come on so strongly. I felt guilty for being so wrapped up in planning my wedding that I didn't have time to see her as often as she would have liked over the last few months. I felt guilty that I didn't say I love you more often, even though I rarely heard it from her. Most of all, I felt enormous guilt for telling the nurse to do nothing that night in the hospital when the nurse asked me what they should do regarding my mother's DNR. Then, of course, comes the anger; angry that the person has been taken from you, angry that you have to deal with all of this. Angry that they never apologized for the wrongs they caused you. Yes, like I said, it was a long, sleepless night.

As the days and weeks passed, so did many milestones. My first holiday without my mother was Thanksgiving, one of her favorites. At this point, I had become so unlike my typical self; I was irrational, emotional, angry and disorganized. I couldn't seem to pull myself together, and the looming holidays only exasperated these new personality traits. It became routine for me to silently sob on a nightly basis until sleep eventually found me. Every time my mind wasn't occupied with something else, and sometimes even when it was, my thoughts would drift to images and memories of my mother and I would fall apart. I remember sobbing hysterically in the shower one morning as I shaved my legs, remembering when I was twelve and decided to shave my legs for the first time and my mother's reaction when I so proudly told her what I had just done. "You know, now you have to always shave," she had said to me. I was living my life, day after day, on auto pilot. I was going through the motions physically present, but emotionally unattached. I remember picking up the phone and calling my mother's house repeatedly, just to hear her voice on the answering machine.

I felt so alone despite the fact that I was surrounded by people. No one understood what I was going through, I convinced myself. My grandmother had just lost her only daughter and it destroyed her, but I couldn't bear to talk to her. My sister, having now lost both of her parents, fell into a deep depression and decided to self-medicate by turning to drugs. She and her boyfriend were living from house to house and no one knew where to find them from one day to the next. Nick had never lost a parent and in fact, we lived with his parents during this time. My soon to be mother-in-law, Karen, lost her mother, but not under circumstances that were anything near similar. My mother, who died at thirty-nine, was younger than Nick's mother. Karen had lost her mother, Katherine, to Alzheimer's when Katherine was in her late 60's, which was still young, but she lived to see her children grow, marry, give her grandchildren and see those grandchildren grow up. My mother was not going to be at my wedding in July and, while she was there for the birth and first year of her first grandson's life, she wouldn't be there to see him grow up or to experience any future grandchildren.

For the first time in my life, I couldn't even turn to my best friend for support because I felt that even she couldn't understand what I was going through; she still had both of her parents after all so, how could she?

Everything seemed to remind me of my mother and the nightmares and flashes of memories weren't helping. A few times, I found myself following people that resembled her until they would turn around and reveal to me that they obviously weren't my dead mother. While out Christmas shopping one day, I followed a car similar to hers, a red Plymouth Horizon hatchback, for several blocks before I realized that the driver was a man. I felt as if I was losing my mind and I fell deeper into depression. The fact that I experienced a miscarriage only a few short weeks prior to my mother's death only exasperated these feelings. I contacted a grief counseling hotline that suggested I find a local support group, but I wasn't interested in sitting amongst a room full of strangers and explaining how I sometimes stalk people in the mall who I think might be my dead mother. That sort of confession typically lands a person a one way ticket to a padded room at the local psychiatric facility.

My soon-to-be in-laws had recently closed on the purchase of a two-family house and wanted Nick and I to rent the first floor apartment from them. We all moved to the new home in late January of 1999. I decided that it was time to pull myself out of this funk and throw myself into the planning of my pending nuptials. My wedding day was set for July 9th and, ready or not, it was quickly approaching. I also decided that in order to move forward there was still one thing left to do and that was to make the trip up to New York and clean out my mother's house once and for all.

Cleaning out her house was a task I previously couldn't bring myself to carry out. I made excuses for not driving back to her upstate New York home: I was busy with the baby, I didn't want to drive through the mountains in the winter, and I needed my sister's help and couldn't locate her. I had a dozen excuses for not following through on this final responsibility, but the truth was that I was procrastinating because of the finality that the task implied. Cleaning out my mother's house, boxing up her life, our life, and either packing it away or giving it away was emotionally unbearable. Now that I had my own space and we were no longer living in cramped quarters with Nick's parents, the time had come for me to stop making excuses. I chose a Saturday, enlisted the help of my soon-to-be brother-in-law, Stephen, reserved a moving truck and made the drive in early February.

The task of sifting through one's life and neatly packing it away is daunting and near impossible for one person to complete, especially over the course of one day.

I had this preconceived notion that if I just got up there and completed the task at hand in one day, just get it over and done with rather than dragging it out over a few weekends, that I could spare myself the emotional overload. Needless to say, I was sadly mistaken. Anyone who has ever had to pack up an entire household knows that this task cannot be accomplished in one day by one person, not even a person as organized, efficient and Type-A as me.

Since I wasn't entirely ready to let go of anything that belonged to my mother, my plan was to pack everything, bring it back to Massachusetts with me and then place it in storage where I could later go through each item carefully when I was emotionally ready. Armed with cardboard boxes, packing tape and Sharpie markers, I set to work packing up the kitchen first. I slowly made my way through each room of the house, throwing away things that were clearly trash and packing everything else. After hours upon hours, Stephen and I decided to call it a day and head back home. There was still so much work left to be done and it became apparent to me, as the day turned into night, that I would have to come back at least one more time and do this again. A few weeks later, Nick and I returned to New York to finish the task. I asked a friend of my mother's to sell certain large items, such as her washer and dryer and other large items of furniture that I had no use for.

Although I was my sister's legal guardian according to my mother's will, my sister was considered an emancipated minor according to New York state law. She was over the age of sixteen, not in high school and, for all intense and purposes, she was living on her own somewhere. I had no legal recourse for forcing her to come to Massachusetts and live with me or another relative. I also had no clue where she and her boyfriend were staying and none of her friends or his family would give me any information on their whereabouts. I packed whatever belongings my sister had left in the house, left them on the covered porch with her name on them, locked the door and walked away from our mother's house for the last time.

It was time to move forward...

"Part of where I'm going, is knowing where I'm coming from" ~Gavin Degraw

Sometimes in life, before we can move forward we must examine our past. Spanish philosopher, poet and novelist George Santayana said, "Those who cannot remember the past are condemned to repeat it." In my opinion, no truer words have ever been spoken. Our pasts are what help to shape us into the human beings we become. From infancy through adulthood, every experience we have impresses itself upon us, whether positive or negative. In the months that passed after the untimely death of my mother, I realized that in order to move forward with the grieving process, I had to face the demons of my past.

To most of the outside world, my childhood was a normal and pleasant one however, to those who truly knew my family, it was anything but. Looking back now, as an adult, it's easy to see the ways in which that period of my life has shaped me into the person, the mother, I am today. As a child I was exposed to divorce, poverty, homelessness, domestic violence, various forms of abuse, drugs and unsavory people to say the least. I remember, as a child, feeling invisible at times or as if I were just a hindrance to the life my mother wished she could lead. That's not to say that there weren't happy times in my childhood, but sometimes it's easier to remember the not so happy events because they have a way of ingraining themselves into our psyches.

My father, just twenty years old, married my mother on December 3, 1977, nearly two months after her eighteenth birthday. Based on the stories that my mother told me growing up, they married simply to escape their unpleasant home lives. My maternal grandmother, a single mom of two children, raised my mother and uncle with the same iron fist method of abuse she experience as a child. My paternal grandmother was a widowed single mother of three and an alcoholic.

My parents thought that by running off to city hall and getting married, they could thumb their noses at their mothers' and escape to adulthood.

Once married, my mother saw it as her duty to keep house and make a home for her husband and future family while my father worked full time in a local factory. Just ten short months after their marriage, I was born. For a short while, my parents strived to be the all-American nuclear family that neither of them had experienced growing up, but six months after my birth, my father informed my mother that he enlisted in the United States Navy and was leaving her and I for good. Three years later, on the grounds of abandonment, their divorce was final.

When I was roughly eighteen months old, my mother rekindled a long lost friendship with a man she knew when she was in junior high school. His name was Billy and, although seven years her senior, he had been harboring feelings for my mother since they were teenagers. Their friendship quickly grew into a loving, committed relationship and on August 13, 1981 my mother gave birth to my younger sister.

Over the years, Billy repeatedly asked my mother to marry him, but she continuously refused. He was a wonderful father to both my sister and I and loved my mother to the ends of the Earth and back. There was nothing this man wouldn't do for his "lady" and his "girls", as he referred to the three of us. While our family life was, for the most part, happy, it was anything but stable. Although there were never two people more meant for each other than Billy and my mother, their relationship was not without its share of complications, specifically the fact that Billy was what is sometimes considered a functioning alcoholic. He was responsible enough to go to work and had a fantastic job in construction. He made sure that the bills were paid and that we always had enough to eat, clothes to wear and shoes on our feet. As responsible as he was however, there was no denying that Billy had a drinking problem. As much as my mother loved him, she couldn't put up with his loud and often obnoxious behavior when he drank, which in turn caused arguments between the two of them. Their arguments often resulted in my mother throwing Billy out of the house, sometimes with the assistance of the police, until he was sober, at which point he was allowed to come back until the next time he would drink and the cycle would begin again. We moved a lot, never staying in one place very long, mostly because the neighbors would complain about the noise from the arguments or Billy's sometimes obscene behavior when he was drinking.

One particularly awful argument between my mother and Billy resulted in my mother, in a fit of fury, screaming that she didn't love him and that he just needed to leave her the fuck alone. And leave he did. He walked away and stayed away, as she wished. About a week or so passed and then my mother received a phone call from my grandmother. As I lay awake in bed eavesdropping on my mother's phone conversation, I heard her scream "NOOOO! You're lying! NO! This isn't funny! No! No! No!" She slammed the phone down and screamed "FFUUUUUUCK!" I had no idea what was going on, but gut instinct told me to stay put where I was and pretend to be sleeping. A moment later I overheard my mother sobbing in the kitchen as her friend, Cindy, tried to console her and figure out what was going on. The phone call from my grandmother was to inform my mother that Billy had committed suicide by hanging himself while in protective custody at the local police station. It was Sunday, May 8, 1988, Mother's Day.

It was evident that my mother felt extreme guilt over the death of Billy. She quickly spiraled into a deep depression and rather than seek help, she self-medicated by adding alcohol to her repartee of illegal drugs, having made the leap from smoking pot and occasionally doing cocaine, to now popping pills, openly hitting the crack pipe on occasion and snorting coke on a regular basis. During much of my childhood, but especially during this period, my mother also appeared to be trying to regain the youth she felt she missed out on by being a wife and mother at such a young age. She would leave my sister and me with various babysitters for a few hours, or sometimes for a weekend, with people we barely knew, people we'd meet in the drive thru at Burger King, while she went out partying. The men that she invited into her life, and into our home, left little to be desired; men who would beat on her or peep at us while we were getting changed and men who just wanted a quick, easy lay and a place to crash. We never stayed at one address long enough to make friends with the neighborhood kids, mostly because the landlord would tell my mother they wanted us gone for one reason or another, whether inability to pay the rent, the fact my mother was part of an escort service or the fact that the police were called all too often to remove yet another boyfriend for domestic assault. At one point, home was the motel room we stayed in, provided to us by the state in order for my mother to receive some sort of public housing assistance because we were homeless and bouncing from one crack head friend to the next. Every dark, damp, mold infested room there was filled with homeless single mothers, most of which were drug addicts or whores. They would all get together and go out for the night, leaving all of us (my sister and I as well as their own children) with either one of the other mothers or with whomever they could get to babysit us. Sometimes, they'd just wait for us all to fall asleep and slip out, leaving a hotel floor full of sleeping children unattended.

About a year after Billy's death, I remember living in a tiny little basement apartment in a nice neighborhood that was located in a desirable section in a city just north of Boston. Life briefly started to resume some sort of normalcy, even if it meant that I had to take on extra responsibilities. My mother, being a single working mother now, counted on me at age nine and a half and in the third grade, to walk from my elementary school to the daycare my sister attended, six city blocks away, every day to pick her up. Every day I would help my sister gather her belongings in her backpack and together, at nine and six years old, we would walk the four city blocks back to our apartment. Once we arrived at home, I was expected to watch my sister, do household chores, do my homework and start dinner before my mother arrived home at approximately 5:30. By today's standards this would be considered some sort of child neglect and perhaps rightfully so. Looking back, yes, it sucked and it caused me to grow up quicker than I should have, but I also learned valuable life lessons. The sense of responsibility and independence that I gained back then has stuck with me as I've grown into adulthood.

During our stay at this particular apartment, my mother was involved in one of her most violent relationships. The man, George, was someone she had known since grade school. Over the years they remained friends and later formed an intimate relationship; he even lived with us at several points in my childhood. But he did not live at this particular place with us. In fact, by this point he and my mother were supposedly over, but we had all heard that before. George grew obsessive and would come by our house in the middle of the night and kick in all of the windows to our basement apartment. Sometimes, breaking the windows was the extent of his behavior (as if that wasn't bad enough), but other times he would climb through one of the windows. Sometimes he'd end up climbing in my bedroom window, other times a kitchen or living room window. My mother filed restraining order after restraining order, but it did nothing. George kept coming back, several times trying to kill her. Finally, we were thrown out and had to move.

No matter where we lived though, there was never time for playing outside with friends. We weren't allowed outside unless my mother was home and by the time she came home from work and we ate dinner, it was dark. "You can see your friends at school," she used to tell me, "After school, you have responsibilities at home." I didn't dare question my mother's reasoning; these days, as much as a glance in the wrong direction would result in a back hand to the head or a smack in the mouth at the least. I remember one time when I was about 8, while my sister and I were in the tub, she hit me across the thigh with a wet washcloth and it left a welt on my leg for a week. I tried my hardest to stay on my best behavior at all times. My grandmother used to tell my sister and me to, "just behave. You're mother has a lot going on and you girls don't realize how lucky you are to have her. Don't get her mad and she won't have to hit you."

As if any parent *has to* hit their child? Statements like this were made to us as if it were our fault that my mother, an adult, couldn't control her anger and impulses. Over the course of my childhood I was hit with anything that happened to be within my mother's reach—shoes, belts, wet wash clothes on bare skin, a closed fist, an open hand, a spatula, a cookie sheet and even had a cordless phone thrown at me, and for any given reason. I've had shoes thrown at me, been hit with spatulas and belts, smacked in the head, face, arm and on the butt, been grabbed by my hair and punched by the person who was supposed to love and protect me.

Despite the constant turmoil at home, I was always an excellent student. Perhaps as a coping mechanism, a way to hide my imperfect home life, I became a perfectionist at home and at school. My room was always spotless, stuffed animals arranged just so according to size, closet neatly organized with clothes grouped together by color and type of clothing (all of the red shirts together, all of the black pants together, etc.), bed always neatly made with hospital corners before leaving for school every morning. I was quiet and well-behaved in school, so much so that the comments section of every report card always read something to the effect of, "a joy to have in class, excellent student, needs to participate more openly in class." I was always the quiet girl in the back of the class (unless forced to sit in the front because of an alphabetical seating chart) who just wanted to do as she was told and blend in. I always disliked having attention brought to myself in class, especially when it required me to go to the chalk board and perform whatever task the teacher had requested. Reading aloud in class, or worse, public speaking of any kind, made me physically ill. It's not that I couldn't perform the tasks being required of me, it was quite the opposite. I could easily write the sixty page report on Austria in the sixth grade, complete with hand drawn, color coded maps and personal interview of a Holocaust survivor, but the thought of having to stand in-front of the class and read it aloud made my palms sweat, heart race and my stomach do back flips.

I feigned ill through most of my school years any time a class presentation was due. Still, I managed to receive all A's in every subject every year. I had to; it was expected of me and nothing less was acceptable in my mother's eyes.

If I came home with anything less than an A on a report card I was grounded, and not just for a week; I was grounded until the next report card came out! What little time I did have for friends or anything else outside of school and household responsibilities was stripped away, for how long I never knew. Some could argue that my mother's constant pushing for me to do my very best and never settle for anything less than an A was her way of teaching me work ethic and that education is important. While that may be true to some extent, I feel that to some degree it was just one more way of controlling me. My younger sister was not held to the high standards that I was when it came to school. It was acceptable for her to receive B's, C's and D's because of her ADHD and the excuse that, "her father committed suicide." There was no pushing or constant pressure from my mother for my sister to do better or try harder the way that there was for me and I always resented that.

Through my elementary school years I attended nine different schools in four cities. I repeated the third grade due to excessive absences and during those two years alone I attended four different schools. To say that making and keeping friends was difficult is an understatement. In the middle of my fifth grade year my mother uprooted my sister and I once again, back to a city we lived in just two years prior. We moved in to the second floor of a two family house on a fairly quiet street in a nice neighborhood. My mother no longer demanded that my sister and I, then eleven and eight, stay inside every day after school until she came home like she did when we were younger. Maybe it was because she trusted us, or maybe it was because she knew the single mom who lived downstairs was home all day and night. Once our chores and homework were done, we were allowed to stay right out in-front of the house with the neighborhood kids. And there were plenty of them! Almost every house for at least three houses in either direction of ours had at least one child our age living in it.

My sister and I had become accustomed to having to make new friends everywhere we went so, making friends in our new neighborhood was not an issue. Before long, summer vacation arrived and we were begging to stay outside long after the street lights came on to play with our friends. Daylight hours were either spent playing kick ball or stick ball in the street or at the beach; one or two moms would pack all of the neighborhood kids in their car (or cars) and we'd head to the local beach for the day. Evening hours were filled with the flicker of flashlights and screams of, "I found you!" during our nightly ritual of flashlight tag, as the mothers looked on, chit chatting from their porches. Finally, we had found a place that felt like home. We lived in a neighborhood where every mother knew the neighborhood children by name and if you were doing something you shouldn't be doing, not only was Mrs. X going to give you a tongue lashing, but she was also going to tell your mother what you'd been up to. Yes, I finally lived in a neighborhood that to me was akin to neighborhoods I had only seen on T.V.

Summer soon faded into fall and before I knew it, another new school year came and went. At some point towards the end of that sixth grade year I met my soul mate, my best friend Danielle. She lived the next street over from me and was attending the same junior high that I was about to attend come fall. Like all kindred spirits, we instantly clicked and before long, we were inseparable. While we didn't share a similar upbringing, we both had mothers who were emotionally detached from their children and that was enough for us to declare ourselves sisters for life. There wasn't anything that Danielle and I didn't know about each other. We spent every waking minute together in and out of school, shared every detail of our lives with each other and trusted each other with every secret. Through fights with friends, our dysfunctional families, new loves and broken hearts, together we shared it all.

In March of our eighth grade school year, my mother informed me that, in an effort to escape yet another abusive boyfriend, we were moving to central Massachusetts. For the next two weeks, like any normal tween girls would, Danielle and I schemed and plotted ways that I could accidentally be left behind.

Finally we concocted what we thought was a fool proof plan: I would move in with Danielle and her family for the remainder of the school year. Both mothers approved and were fully on board with our plan until my mother learned that she'd have to sign over legal guardianship of me to Danielle's parents in case of an emergency. This was a deal breaker for my mother; she was willing to let me move in with Danielle's family for the next three months so that I could finish the school year, but not if it meant relinquishing even the tiniest bit of parental power over me. A few short weeks later, after a very teary goodbye between Danielle and me, my mother packed us up and moved us an hour away.

Our new neighborhood, with its perfectly manicured lawns and quaint Ozzy and Harriet feeling, was in a city with very distinctly segregated neighborhoods. Our new address was located in a neighborhood that consisted of mostly Middle-class families and older folks who stayed in the homes where they raised their families long after their children had grown and gone. Unfortunate for me, the middle school in this section of town was not accepting any new students so late in the year and I was forced to attend the school on the other side of town, the less desirable section of town. Due to safety concerns, my mother allowed me to practically be homeschooled without actually withdrawing me from school. I would attend school on Monday, receive the homework for every class, stay home for the rest of the week and go back on Friday to turn in my work. Once I made a couple of friends, I would sometimes attend three days a week just to see my friends. I managed to survive the final three months of eighth grade and somehow I graduated despite the excessive absences.

My mother reluctantly agreed to let me attend the local vocational school rather than the public high school. The way I figured, we'd likely move again sometime soon so I might as well get some job training and skills under my belt while I can. I started ninth grade and loved every minute of it. School was a welcome distraction from my everyday home life. I quickly made new friends and, being a typical teenager, began dating. This new phase of my life must have frightened my mother for so many reasons: she knew the dangers of young love, but more importantly she was losing control of me little by little.

Despite never having given my mother a reason not to trust me, I felt smothered by her lack of trust and her complete disregard for privacy. She ransacked my bedroom on a daily basis while I was at school. She listened in on every phone call, read every note I passed in school or that was passed to me and when friends came over we had to stay within ear shot of her. She was not only convinced that I was doing something wrong, she constantly accused me and was determined to find proof to support her suspicions. Her accusations and constant surveillance made me want to push the envelope and see how much I could get away with. The way I figured it, I was already getting screamed at, hit and punished for things she thought I was doing and wasn't so I might as well do something worth getting punished for. I started making up stories about why I needed to stay at my friend's and boyfriend's houses, saying that a parent or his much older brother was taking us to the drive-in and since it would be so late when the three movies were over and his grandfather would be there all night, can't I just stay in the spare bedroom? Truth be told, we rarely went to the drive-in, his grandfather worked overnight, his older brothers were the ones supplying us with alcohol and there was so spare bedroom.

During the summer between ninth and tenth grade, my father made a halfhearted attempt to pop back into my life by asking my mother if I could stay with him in upstate New York for a week in July. I was nearly fifteen at the time and it had been about four years since I had last seen him. Back then his reason for taking me for a week was to introduce me to my stepmother, stepbrother and half-brother, so I was a little cautious about who or what this unexpected trip was about. Contrary to my teenage fears, the trip went quite well and seemed to be the beginning of trying to repair our estranged relationship.

By the time I turned fifteen, I was testing boundaries a little more openly with my mother, flexing my new found confidence and exerting a little independence. One February evening, my mother and I got into a heated argument over a note between a friend and I in which I confided a childhood trauma. I had been having increased nightmares which caused me to continuously relive the horrific sexual abuse I suffered at the hands of someone my mother considered a very dear friend who had recently passed away. This man's passing brought about such relief within me that I felt such immense guilt at first, until I began to vividly remember and recount the disgusting things he did to me beginning when I was eight years old and ending about just after I turned eleven and got my first period. When my mother read the words I had written to my friend, making this confession, she was beyond irate...at me! My biggest fear had come true, my own mother believed my attacker rather than believing me. She called me a liar and a slut, told me that I must be having sex and I just want to hide it by accusing an innocent person of horrific things. She told me I needed to be committed for making up such sick stories. She told me I was nothing but a filthy tramp. I became so infuriated that when she swung to smack me in the face for telling what she considered to be bold faced lies, rather than wince as I normally would, I grabbed her hand and told her that she better think twice before hitting me. The expression of shock that came over her face very quickly turned to rage in a matter of seconds. She raised her other hand in a clench fist and before I could react, her fist landed on my cheekbone. When I realized that I was a split second too late in raising my hands to protect myself, I ended up shoving her hands off of me and telling her to go fuck herself. I thought she was going to kill me, but instead she threw me against the wall, smacked me a couple more times, screamed a few obscenities at me, told me to stop being such a little whore, dished out a lifelong punishment and stormed down the stairs and out of my room.

The next day, sporting a black eye and bruised cheekbone (both of which were very difficult to conceal even with makeup) and a backpack full of clothes and school books, I started asking friends if I could go home with them because I couldn't go home. After cheerleading practice, I very calmly called my mother from the school pay phone and informed her that I would not be home because I felt we both needed time to cool off. I told her whose house I was going to and gave her the phone number. She began screaming and I calmly told her that we could talk about what happened when she calmed down, which she refused, so I said goodbye and hung up. Once I got to my friend's house, I called my father in New York and told him what had happened, which of course, he already knew because my mother had called him to inform him what a little bitch of a daughter he had created and left her with. I asked, and then begged, to live with him and he refused, telling me to work things out with my mother. Feeling rejected and unloved by both of my parents, I had no choice but to go home the next day after school and live with the consequence she doled out— grounded indefinitely.

My mother's definition of grounded consisted of no contact with the outside world other than at school, and sometimes even school was outlawed. I was driven to and from school rather than being allowed to take the school bus as I normally would. This also meant no phone calls, not even to family members, and certainly no T.V. Depending on her level of rage it wasn't unheard of for meals to be eaten in solitude. My backpack and pockets were checked upon all arrivals and departures. My bedroom was ransacked and everything I owned, every nook and cranny, was gone over with a fine toothed comb on a daily basis. She did everything short of strip searching and cavity checks, but did threaten full body inspections if she felt it was necessary.

Over the course of the next few months, my mother realized that her abusive relationship with her on again off again live-in boyfriend, Steve, needed to end once and for all and the only way to make that happen was to disappear. She and my father had been talking a great deal recently and they had decided that, after nearly sixteen years of being apart, they were going to try and rekindle what they once had. This epiphany meant packing up and moving once again, this time to upstate New York. I was about to enter my junior year of high school and once again, my mother's needs and desires were put ahead of what was best for my sister and I. At least that's how it always felt.

Once we were settled in to our new home in our new town (so small that it wasn't even on the map) school began. Two weeks into the new school year and my guidance counselor wanted to meet with me to see how I was adjusting and discuss my plans for senior year. During my meeting with the counselor I learned that I only needed two credits the following year in order to graduate. The wheels in my head began turning and when I suggested to the counselor, a man who had never met me until now, that instead of wasting time in study halls most of my senior year I take those two credits now and graduate a year early, I thought I was speaking in a foreign tongue for a second. He looked at me with such an expression of confusion that, had there been a thought bubble over his head like in comic strips, it would have read "Huh??" In the end, with my parents' approval, I was allowed to do just that and I was on the path to graduate from high school one year early at age sixteen and a half. By December, my parents' ill attempt at rekindling whatever they thought they had failed and my father moved out, resuming his previous role as absentee parent.

Now, deep down I had ulterior motives for doubling up my junior and senior years of high school and graduating at sixteen—I learned that once I turned sixteen, and could support myself, I was considered an emancipated minor according to the State of New York. During the course of the school year I had already applied for and been accepted to multiple colleges, secured full financial aid and had means of supporting myself. I was about to be completely free from my mother's control for the first time in my life and I couldn't wait! I graduated the first week of June in 1995 and by the end of June I was sitting in my dorm room at my chosen school. I was free! Or so I thought.

Nearly every day during that summer semester, my mother called to tell me how much trouble she was having with my sister and how she wasn't feeling well. The other half of the calls were spent dictating to me what I was and was not allowed to do, with whom and what the consequences would be if she found out I had disobeyed her. Even from over 300 miles away my mother was still trying to micromanage, and control, my every move by using guilt and then threats. For years my mother had pushed me to do better, be better, pursue college and now that I was doing it she was threatening, "I'll drive out there and come get your ass if you don't do what the fuck I say." Her reasons for wanting me home were not the typical "my-child-is-all-grown-up-and-gone" grieving process most, if not all, parents go through when their child reaches this stage of life. No, she was driven out of pure selfishness and lack of control. "You're sister doesn't listen and nothing is being done around here while I'm at work," "Having to work and take care of the house and your sister is wearing on me physically, I can't do this anymore," "I think you should go to a different school so that you can be home doing what you should be doing here which is helping me with your sister and the house." "I know that you're just off being a little whore instead of studying so why do you even need to be there?" By the end of September, just a few short weeks into the fall semester of my freshman year, I succumbed to the emotional and mental harassment, took a leave of absence and went home to help her. Unfortunately, my temporary leave of absence became permanent and I never did return to finish my degree.

A few months later, winter was upon us, and we had all returned to our old routines: Ma would go off to work every morning after leaving a to-do list for my sister and I, my sister would complain about how unfair it was that she had to get up and go to school and I didn't, and I would take care of the housework and go to work. One December night, while hanging out with my step-brother and some friends, it began snowing heavily. None of us had cars and walking on pitch black, windy country roads in a snow storm wasn't exactly safe. Knowing that I still had a strictly enforced curfew, I called my mother and asked for a ride home. She outright refused and told me she didn't care how I got home, but my ass better be in that house by 11:00 or else she was locking the door and "don't bother coming home" were her exact words. "There's no way I will be home by 11 in this weather even if I find a ride!" I responded, but she wasn't hearing it. "Then don't bother coming home…EVER!" And with that statement my mother was calling my bluff. Either I walked home, which would have easily been an hour long walk in good weather and I'd still miss curfew and arrive home to a locked door, or I stayed put and went home in the morning. I chose to stay put, ride out the storm and go home in the morning, and I called to let her know this, but she refused to answer the phone. When morning arrived, word got around that I didn't come home the night before because my mother contacted every single one of my friends and told them what a whore I was and that if they saw me to let me know that I was not to come back to her house. I had just turned seventeen and had no clothes or belongings other than what I was wearing and I now had no home to return to.

For the next month or so I stayed at a couple different friends' homes before I finally contacted my maternal grandmother and asked her if I could come to Massachusetts and live with her. A few weeks later, in January of 1996, my grandmother took the three and a half hour trip alone to pick me up and took me home to live with her. My mother never attempted to contact me despite her full knowledge of where I was.

Until August of that year...

"We cannot change the past, but we can change our attitude toward it. Uproot guilt and plant forgiveness. Tear out arrogance and seed humility. Exchange love for hate – thereby making the present comfortable and the future promising." ~Maya Angelou

It was a typical New England summer day in August of 1996: a perfect combination of brutally humid, heavy air mixed with blazing sun. Ironically, this was the sort of day my mother loved. It also happened to be the day that, for the first time since January, my grandmother was contacted by my mother. My grandmother handed the letter to me, assuming that it was truly meant for me and that this was just my mother's stubborn attempt at contacting me without *really* contacting me. My mother ranted for pages about how she couldn't believe that her own mother would turn on her and side with me, about how I was nothing but a spoiled and ungrateful child who deserved to have nothing. About three quarters of the way through the letter she explained that she has been sick for a long time, how her health has taken a turn for the worse and she's not getting better, and how she never will. The shocking conclusion to what appeared to be a halfhearted attempt at reconciliation was when she confessed that the reason she knew she would never recuperate is because she had just been diagnosed with HIV.

My jaw dropped as I read that line silently to myself, repeatedly, each time my heart sinking further into the pit of my chest and my stomach becoming more violently ill. I saw the words on the page, in my mother's clear and distinct handwriting and yet I could not for the life of me comprehend what I was reading. When I finally regained the ability to think, my first instinct was to pick up the phone and call her, which is exactly what I did.

It was a very awkward phone call, the first time we had spoken to each other in over six months and it was only because I just read that she was terminally ill. In hind sight, it's pretty sad that it took being diagnosed with a terminally ill disease for the two of us to put away our stubbornness and reconnect. The initial awkwardness wore off after several minutes and the discussion quickly went to one of me seeking information from her and passing along what knowledge I had gained during high school sex education classes courtesy of Planned Parenthood. By the end of the conversation, which lasted approximately twenty minutes, it was as if nothing had happened.

My mother and I never spoke of the events that led to my living with my grandmother or of our nearly nine months with no communication with one another. My mother was never one to discuss problems and try to reach a solution, nor was she the type of person to apologize. Issues in our family were simply swept under the rug and everyone acted as if nothing ever happened. Growing up I never liked this game since I wasn't very good at forgetting or letting go of my hurt feelings, but over time I learned how to bury my feelings deep inside and tried my best to play along according to the rules. As an adult, I'm a pro at never letting my true feelings show.

Over the next couple of months my mother and I spoke on the phone often, usually about recent visits to the doctor which included updates about her T-cell count, weight issues, side effects from the HIV antiviral "cocktail" medications, symptoms she was having and anything else she had discussed with the doctor. During this period, my mother and I began putting the pieces of what little relationship we ever had back together. In our own, twisted way, we put aside the stubbornness and replaced it with some semblance of forgiveness, or at least forgetfulness. Whatever it was, we each decided to move on and not look back.

In January of 1997, just five months after learning of my mother's diagnosis, I became violently ill. What started out feeling like a cold, progressed into feeling like I had the flu. I was achy, beyond nauseous, couldn't eat, slept for twelve or more hours and still felt exhausted, and would feel faint and pass out any time I was in a vertical position. Around week four of feeling this way, my mind began to play the What If game-- What if this isn't the flu? What if there's something seriously wrong with me? What if my mother somehow, inadvertently infected me? What if it was something else? I made an appointment to see my doctor and I asked her to test me for everything and anything she could think of. I explained that I was currently working with the public and I knew that there was a new and strange version of chicken pox that was going around so, please test me for that. I also informed her that my mother recently tested positive for H.I.V so she might as well test me for that while she was at it. Oh and since I've been sick for weeks now, perhaps testing me for mono, leukemia and anything else she could think of might be useful as well. I assure you, I am not a hypochondriac, but I am certain I sounded like one that day!

After fainting in the elevator on my way back to the car, I made it back home and back to bed, hoping that more rest and fluids was the only cure I needed. Two days later, I went back to my doctor for my results. She read down the list of ailments that resulted in negative test results: I was not H.I.V positive. I did not have the chicken pox (and in fact I tested positive for antibodies so, I was now immune to them). I was not suffering from mono nor was I suffering from any type of cancer or other known disease. The only test that came back positive was my pregnancy test. What?!

Now, being that I was a fairly intelligent eighteen year old young lady with basic knowledge of how the reproductive system works, I was certain that there was absolutely no way on Earth that I could possibly be pregnant. For one thing, I was on the pill and secondly, I had taken five home pregnancy tests in December when my period was two weeks late and they *all* came up negative! How could I possibly be pregnant? The doctor smirked at me as if to say "stupid child" and then assured me that I was in fact pregnant. She performed an ultrasound and there on the screen was the tiniest little baby with the strongest little heartbeat. She determined that I was roughly ten weeks along and gave me a list of obstetricians that she recommended.

Pregnant?! Of all of the words, all of the diagnosis that I expected to hear from my doctor's mouth, pregnant was certainly not one of them. It took me a little while to wrap my head around this news and once I did, the first person I told was my mother. Terrified, I dialed her number and once she answered I sprung the news on her. My mother's only response was "OK...um...OK...um...I need to sit down...OK...I'm going to be a grandmother at 37...OK...um...I need to call you back." I anxiously waited for what seemed like an eternity for her to call me back, fifteen minutes later the phone rang.

My mother handled the news of my pregnancy and her becoming a grandmother quite well, much better than I anticipated actually, from that point on. She took me to doctor appointments, was with me for the ultrasound when I learned that I was having a boy, went shopping with me a couple of times and helped my grandmother plan a baby shower for me. When my hormones and emotions were running high and I called her hysterically crying because I was overwhelmed or frustrated, she would make the three and a half hour drive from upstate New York to Massachusetts and pick me up for a much needed mini vacation.

In some weird way, being a mother-to-be changed my relationship with her. I suddenly had the mother-daughter relationship, or at least some form of it, that I had always dreamed of, but only seen on T.V. or read about in books. We talked almost daily on the phone, each sharing our symptoms and ailments, and updating each other on other events in our daily lives. I confided in her that Nick was driving me up a wall by hovering over me, following me around like a lost puppy dog every time I moved and she told me my father was the same way when she was pregnant with me. "When I was pregnant with you, your father and Grandma drove me bat shit crazy! I used to have to lock myself in the bathroom and run all of the water to drown them out, just to get few minutes to myself and calm down. You should try it. All of that stress isn't good for the baby. And you tell him I said to leave you the fuck alone or I'll come down there and kick his ass. That's my grandson in there!"

The change in our relationship was awkward and uncomfortable at times, maybe not for her, though I can't be certain, but I know it was for me. I wasn't used to my mother hugging me or saying anything kind. I wasn't used to trusting her with my thoughts and feelings. I wasn't used to depending on her for support or advice. I never dressed up in her high heels and put on her lipstick in an effort to "be just like Mommy", because being in her room and touching her things was a huge no-no, punishable by spanking and screaming. We were never best friends, or even friendly at all. In our house she was the authority figure and that was that. There was no warmth, no affection.

Now, here we were in this place where we were sharing details of our lives, sharing thoughts and feelings, confiding in each other to some extent. But we were doing it in an awkward and almost forced way, sort of like we knew this was how we should behave. Throughout my pregnancy, my mother and I spent a lot of time together. We weren't *re*building a mother-daughter relationship, we were building one.

I felt like I finally had a mom, rather than a warden who I was entrusted to. Through morning sickness that lasted for several months, to OB/GYN visits, to the ultrasound that revealed that I was having a boy, to choosing names and shopping for supplies, my mother was there for all of it. She offered me tips and tricks for combatting my horrible morning sickness. She was thrilled to be having a grandson and offered up suggestions for names, saying "Just don't pick anything too guido-

Italian. The poor kid will sound like he just came off the boat!" She helped me register for baby supplies, telling me what was useful and which items were really wastes of money. "No one ever uses those baby wash clothes, but if you happen to get them as a gift you can use them as burp clothes."

It was amazing and strange all at the same time. This behavior was so unlike anything I had experience with my mother that I was constantly waiting for the proverbial other shoe to drop. I was waiting for her to take all of the support and niceness away if I said the wrong thing or didn't agree with her. I had periods of just living in the moment and enjoying the time with her, followed by moments where I'd pull back and be on my best behavior, minding my P's and Q's and being a good little girl who had no opinion about anything. After all, that's how I was conditioned to act.

I had a rather stressful, but uneventful pregnancy up until I hit the 34 week mark.

If ever there was a true test of this new found relationship between my mother and me, this just might have been it...

Mothers and daughter become closest when daughters become mothers.
~unknown

"You're in the home stretch so when your due date gets closer, I'll come down and stay until the baby is born. This way I can take you to the hospital and make sure Nick doesn't faint." This was the conversation between my mother and me one July afternoon. I gave my mother a quick call just to check in with an update on baby shower guests before Nick and I headed to his parents' house for Sunday dinner.

I was 34 weeks pregnant and, having suffered through debilitating morning sickness that lasted all day, every day for nearly seven months, I finally felt great. I had only gained an additional eight pounds past my pre-pregnancy weight, but that's because I had to re-gain the thirteen pounds I had lost in the first and second trimesters. The dizziness was subsiding for the most part, but I still couldn't drive or be left alone for fear of hurting myself if I were to faint (which I had been doing throughout my pregnancy).

Nick and I had a lovely Sunday dinner with his parents, siblings, aunt, cousin and grandparents, in true Italian style. Pasta, meatballs, chicken parmesan, desserts; you name it and it was probably on that table. Of course, everyone was trying to get me to keep eating, worried that I wasn't "big enough." "You're eating for two, keep eating!" Stuffed to the gills, we left Nick's family that night, taking leftovers with us, and headed back to my Grandmother's so I could get some sleep.

Around 2:00 AM, I awoke with terrible heartburn. Being that this is a typical pregnancy ailment, especially late in pregnancy and given that I had gorged myself on delicious Italian food all afternoon, I waddled to the kitchen for a tall glass of milk and some Tums before heading back to bed. But the uncomfortable feeling was now progressing into pain. I tried to walk, I tried to sit up, I tried to lie down; nothing helped and the pain just kept getting worse. After an hour of trying to cope, and the pain getting worse by the minute, I decided that I better call the doctor, and I was told to come in to labor and delivery to be checked out. I woke my grandmother up to drive me, called Nick (waking his dad who answered the phone) and asked him to meet us. I didn't know what was going on, but I wanted him to be there.

Once I got settled in, the nurse hooked me up to the monitor and saw that I was having contractions. They gave me a shot of Terbutaline, a medication that is meant to stop contractions, and hooked me up to an I.V. At this point I decided that I'm probably looking at an overnight hospital stay and I better call my mother to let her know what was happening. "I just got home from work, but I'm on my way!" I never expected her to jump in the car at 3:30 in the morning and drive 3 ½ hours to Boston, especially when we still had no idea if this was even something to worry about.

The first shot of Terbutaline didn't work so I was given a second shot. When that didn't work, and I was still contracting, I had to be rushed by ambulance to New England Medical Center, a hospital with a neo-natal intensive care unit and, therefore, better equipped to handle premature babies should they be unable to stop my labor.

Now I was panicking! Premature baby? Neo-natal intensive care unit? I'm not ready to give birth and this baby still needs time to cook. Neither of us is ready! For the first time since I was probably about 3 years old, I thought to myself, "I want my mommy!"

By the time my mother arrived in Boston, I was already at New England Med, hooked up to a ton of machines, being briefed by every doctor and nurse in the NICU, as they tried to assure me that they were doing everything possible to keep this baby in utero for a few more weeks. My mother questioned the doctors and nurses, wanting to know everything that was being done and to be sure they were doing everything possible. She was also there as a buffer between Nick and I, who was overcome with excitement over the pending birth, rather than the fear of his child being born with defects due to a premature birth. His elation was annoying the hell out of me as I lay there writhing in pain from contraction after contraction.

Eventually, my mother strongly suggested to Nick that he go home and sleep, to which he obliged us both and left. The entire ordeal ended up with me in the NICU for 24 hours of observation; labor eventually stopped and I was allowed to go home on complete bed rest for the remainder of my pregnancy.

For the next six weeks I was climbing the walls. I am not a person to sit still and do nothing, or to let people do things for me, so it was driving me to the brink of insanity to just stay in bed and do nothing, especially since this was how I spent the first several months of my pregnancy due to illness. The thought that I may never put myself through this again crossed my mind more than once. Was this whole horrible pregnancy ordeal really worth it? And then of course I felt horrible for even thinking such thoughts. Then, one Tuesday night, two days before my due date, while watching Beverly Hills 90210 with Nick, I began to have slight contractions. I had been to the doctor the day before and, the doctor covering for my own doctor, decided to "separate the membranes" to try and push me into active, natural labor. Separating the membranes requires the doctor, during an internal vaginal exam, to sweep their finger around the cervix between the cervix and the amniotic sack. For some women, this is enough to naturally induce labor; I can be counted in that "some women' category.

As Nick and I sat there watching TV, I silently took notice of the twinges I was having, not overly concerned since I did have his mother's sauce that day and it could just be heartburn. As the show went on, I grew more and more uncomfortable; both Nick and my grandmother could see it on my face. At this point, the pains I was feeling were about

5 and a half minutes apart. I decided to call my mother, who had run to the store briefly, and let her know. I also called the doctor and was told to come in.

I arrived at the hospital sometime just after 9 pm and was checked in to labor and delivery. In the short car ride to the hospital, I remember begging my mother to give me whatever pain meds she had in her purse, to which she laughed at me and said, "You can do this." I didn't believe her at the time. How on Earth was I going to get through pushing this thing out of *there* if it already hurt like this now?!

Once I was situated in the bed, hooked up to the fetal heart monitor, and checked out by the nurses and doctor, things progressed pretty quickly. With my mother on my right, Nick on my left, and my younger sister pacing the floor at the foot of the bed trying not to look, I labored and delivered a healthy baby boy. After six and a half hours of labor, Zachary Aaron Vozzella was born just one day before his due date, with a full head of dark brown hair and deep, dark brown eyes. My mother was there to witness the birth of her first grandchild and she couldn't wait to hold him. You could see on her face that she loved that little baby to pieces. For a fleeting moment, I wondered if she had ever looked at me that way.

The next few weeks were spent focusing on the move: Nick and I were moving up to New York to stay with my mother. She was going to help us with the baby, and I was going to help her with the house and my sister now that her health was taking a turn for the worse. She didn't have the strength of the energy to do half of what she was trying to do. The H.I.V cocktail meds made her nauseous and she had some memory loss. She also began having seizures and needed monitoring. She was still working as much as she could and trying to hold things together as best she could. But she needed help.

Living with my mother again, in her house, took its toll on me, and on Nick. My mother had certain expectations and Nick just didn't live up to them. Quite frankly, he wasn't living up to mine either. I was working a part time job and coming home to take care of the baby; he on the other hand was barely capable of boiling water and left my mother to take care of the baby. This annoyed the hell out of my mother and she let him know on a constant basis that this was his kid, not hers, and he had to step up and be a man.

Nick grew impatient with my mother, but never spoke up. He also grew impatient with the baby, and that's when he and I began to break down. Our relationship just wasn't what it once was and now we had this beautiful three month old son who needed a father, and Nick just wasn't stepping up. We constantly fought; he constantly accused me of having an affair with old high school friends despite the fact that I only left the house for work and nothing else. He missed his family and wanted to go home; I felt we were his family now and he needed to man up. (Not to say that he couldn't visit them, he could! And he spoke to them every day, a few times a day, on the phone.)The strain turned into resentment for each other and finally he decided to leave New York and move back home to his parents in Massachusetts. In a last ditch effort to salvage any relationship we still had left, Nick asked me to marry him, and I said no. I couldn't fathom the idea of marrying someone who had so much resentment for me. Why, to appease his family? That's not a good enough reason and he just got done telling me he can't stand me, that he doesn't love me and that the only reason he stayed with me is because I was pregnant! What girl wants to run to the alter after such a romantic display of emotion?!

And now I was in the exact place I never wanted to be: I was a young, single mother; I had become my mother.

"It has been said that time heals all wounds, I do not agree. The wounds remain. In time, the mind, protecting its sanity, covers them with scar tissue, and the pain lessens, but is never gone." ~Rose Kennedy

It's been 15 years since my mother's passing and still it feels like just yesterday. So much has happened in such a relatively short amount of time. She has missed so much, and I have missed having her there to share it with me.

She has missed seeing her first grandchild grow into a warm, sarcastic, caring, handsome young man. Though she was alive for the reconciliation between Nick and I six months after our split, and for our engagement, she died 8 months before our wedding. She missed the birth of my younger three children, as well as the birth of my sister's only son and her wedding. She's missed my divorce after 11 years of marriage, and me finding myself, even if it didn't happen until my 30's.

There have been so many times over the past 15 years when I wished I could call her, talk to her, see her, ask her advice or opinion, or just hear her tell me to grow the fuck up because it was what I needed to hear at that moment.

Then of course I think of all of the unfinished business between the two of us. I feel as if as soon as she and I started to connect and have any semblance of a mother-daughter relationship, she was taken away from me. As if the universe were thumbing its nose at me and saying, "Nah-nah-nah-nah-nah, here's what you missed your entire childhood, but psych! You can't keep it! HA HA!"

There are so many important reasons why a woman needs her mother, and I feel like I have missed out on all of them. I never learned how to form healthy relationships with women, mostly because I didn't have it modeled for me and partly because I didn't have that most important female relationship in my life: the one between mother and daughter. I also never really learned to form healthy male-female relationships because of the unhealthy ones that were modeled for me. Besides, how can you ever really love someone else if you can't love and accept yourself? There are so many things about my childhood that I am ashamed of, that I've never really opened up to anyone about them, ever. No one knows I was homeless most of my childhood. No one knows the true extent of the physical, emotional and verbal abuse I suffered. Less than a handful of people know about the sexual abuse I endured, though none know the details. Aside from my maternal grandmother, no one knows the domestic violence that I was subjected to; watching my mother being beaten, of having the life nearly choked out of her by boyfriend after boyfriend. No one knows how I spent the majority of my childhood going to state prisons to visit these so-called boyfriends with my mother.

I have sought counseling a few times; I've never found it to really work, maybe because of my inability to truly trust and open up. I know I can't blame my mother, or our limited relationship for all of my personality quirks, but I can't help but wonder: if I had a better relationship with her, would I still be the woman I am today?

I've had 15 years to grow up and to truly reflect on my life. Did I have the best, or even a good, childhood? No, not by any means, but I made it through alive in spite of my circumstances. I didn't become a statistic; having grown up in a single parent household, in poverty and homelessness, with drugs, alcohol and abuse present, I made it out in one piece and as an upstanding citizen. I'm not an addict, I've never been in trouble with the law for anything more than a traffic ticket, I'm educated and I stopped the cycle of abuse.

Examining my relationship with my mother, the only parental figure in my life growing up is an ongoing process. When I was pregnant with my oldest child, I really questioned whether I should be a parent at all. How could I possibly mother a child when I had nothing from my own childhood to pull from? Being a woman without a mother is hard enough, but being a mother without a mother? It's not something I would wish for others to experience.

But I've done it. I don't think I could be the mother I am today if she wasn't the mother she was. I've paved my own way, made my own choices, and inevitably my own mistakes as well.

"Mistake, I've made a few…" Frank Sinatra, My Way

Nick and I were doomed from the start. I was 17 and he was 18 when we began dating in June of 1996. We both worked at the same grocery store as cashiers and flirted with each other on a daily basis. Things moved very quickly between us and after only 5 months of dating, I found out I was pregnant.

His family pushed him to marry me and he kept asking me, but at the urging of my mother, I kept saying no to his proposals. As much as I wanted the fairy tale family, I wanted to be as sure as I could be that he was marrying me for love and not simply because I was pregnant with his child. Fast forward to May of 1998, after the birth of our son Zachary, and a six month separation from each other, Nick and I reconciled. On July 3rd of that year, while away on vacation, he proposed to me yet again. This time I said yes.

I didn't feel the way I thought I would feel, the way I thought I *should* feel. There were no tears, no emotional outburst of any sort. He asked, I was yes, and that was that. It was all very business-like. I know we smiled; I think we hugged. All in all it was more of a "well our son is already a year old, so we might as well just do it" sort of a feeling about it. No one should enter marriage feeling this way, but we did. Honestly, I felt it was the right thing to do for our son. He deserved to have a family with two parents in the same house. He deserved to have everything I wanted growing up, and damn it, I was going to give it to him no matter what the cost! Sure, I loved Nick. He was the father of my child; of course I had loving feelings for him. But I never had the head over heels, knock me off my feet, can't live without you, mushy love feelings that you read about in books or see in movies. In fact, I never said the words 'I Love You' to him. He would tell me all the time and I would respond by smiling and saying 'ditto' or 'me too.'

I wasn't really excited about telling people we were engaged. I didn't rush to the phone and call everyone I knew. Honestly I wanted us to set a date together privately and then let immediate family members know and that's it. I was certainly in no rush to tell my mother. Petrified was more like it.

When we returned from vacation, a friend of my sister noticed the engagement ring on my finger and began asking questions before shouting, "Oh my god! Congratulations you guys!" I froze and my heart nearly beat out of my chest as I awaited my mother's reaction to the news. "Hmph. Why the hell would you go and do something stupid like that?" Not exactly the reaction every girl hopes her mother will have to the news she is engaged, but it was better than it could have been I suppose.

As the days and weeks turned to months, my mother came around to the idea of Nick and me getting married. She began throwing her unsolicited opinion into the mix and trying to help with the wedding plans. She still wasn't thrilled with the idea, but at least she was attempting to be supportive. She visited venues with me, helped me shop for dresses for the girls, and helped me make a guest list.

Then her health took a turn for the worse. She was having more and more seizures, especially since I had moved back to Massachusetts a few months after my engagement. I spoke with Nick and insisted on moving the wedding date back; there was no way I could wait two years and risk my mother not making it to my wedding. Instead of July of 2000, we moved the wedding to July 9, 1999.

The last detail my mother was able to complete with me was picking up my wedding dress. I picked it out on my own with my maid of honor and childhood friend, Danielle. When I went back to pick it up I brought with me Danielle, my mother, and Karen, Nick's mother. I tried it on for them: a fitted, mermaid style, diamond white gown with wide tank straps and gorgeous bead work on the bodice and chapel length train. I wore matching opera length gloves and an elbow length veil. With my wedding still 9 months away, this was the first time anyone, with the exception of Danielle, had seen my dress. Little did I know on that brisk October day that it would be the only time my mother would see me in my dress.

Despite my mental state after my mother died, I went ahead with me wedding. I couldn't bear to let go of anything that reminded me of her, and Nick served as that reminder. I had withstood all of the change I could handle, and I was not about to start letting people down now by changing or postponing the wedding. The show must go on, right?

After all, I had made a promise to this man to marry him. We have a son together. It's the right thing to do, right? Despite my fears and doubts, I put on my big girl panties, walked down the aisle with my godfather, Great Uncle Walt, on my arm and took care of business. We said our 'I do's' in a little gazebo at a hall in Nahant, overlooking the beach at sunset and then went inside for our reception with our guests. As we walked up the stairs to our reception, before the DJ announced us, I paused briefly at the lit memorial candle I had made baring a picture of my mother, Nick and I at our baby shower. (That candle sits on top of my entertainment center to this day.)

Married life did not come easily for me. I had this picture perfect image in my head of how it was "supposed" to be, but I had no real experience to draw from. Nick's parents had been married for 29 years at this point, and he had never known anything else. Both sets of grandparents stayed married for 40 years or more, or until death parted them. I felt pressure to live up to that standard, no matter how real or imagined that pressure was; I felt the weight on my shoulders. Nick wanted a very traditional family life: mom stays home with the children while dad works to provide for the family. Wife keeps house and maintains the home, and husband is simply the provider. Being that I was 20 and wanted to please my new family, I gave in. I quit my job as an assistant teacher in a local preschool program and stayed home with our son full-time. 10 months later, after several miscarriages and thinking we would never have another child; Brendon Nicholas was born in July of 2000, just a few weeks after our first wedding anniversary.

In those early days and weeks after Brendon was born, I found myself yearning for my mother, wishing that she were there to help me, to give me advice on balancing two children. Nick had missed so much of Zachary's infancy that he was like a first time dad all over again. It didn't help matters that Brendon was suffering from food allergies and gastro-intestinal reflux disorder (GERD), causing him to scream uncontrollably for hours on end; and resulting in very little sleep for Nick and I. Nick made half-hearted attempts every now and then to help with the kids, but the child rearing lay primarily on my shoulders. With a screaming infant and a rambunctious 3 year old, life was not very pleasant and neither was I. But Nick wanted to try for that daughter he had always wanted, and as quickly as it was a thought, I was pregnant with baby number three.

When we were young(er) and naïve, we discussed having a big family. But now, in the throes of it all... what the hell were we thinking? More importantly what the hell was I thinking?!

In February of 2002, exactly six months to the day after the 9/11 attacks, our daughter Gianna Cristine was born. Nick and I were now the parents of three children under the age of 6. To say that this put a strain on our relationship is an understatement, but we hadn't really had a great relationship in years at this point. Everyone kept saying it was because we were stressed, overworked, the parents of three young children, overtired; everyone had a list of excuses to offer us, but no real solutions.

Nick and I went about living almost separate lives: he was always at work into the wee hours of the night, and I was always busy with the house, kids and being a mom. Anytime I would make even a slightly romantic gesture towards him— a touch, a kiss, a card, a glass of wine under the stars in the backyard when the kids were in bed— it was shrugged off; intimacy was not important to him, and forget sex! There were so many times I would lay awake wondering if this really was what marriage was supposed to be. Are you really supposed to be completely selfless and just accept that this is adult life?

When I compared my marriage to the only family model I had, my own childhood, I would go down a checklist:

- Is my life or my safety in danger?
- Are my children's lives or safety in danger
- Do we have a roof over our heads?
- Do we have food in our stomachs?
- Do we have clean clothes, warm beds, heat and the basic necessities?
- Will my children be better off if we split up?

At this point in our marriage, the children and I were not in any danger, we had a roof over our heads, food, clothes and all of the basic necessities we needed. But that last question really weighed heavily on me. I absolutely refused to become my mother; I would not easily give up on my family and walk away from my husband, or let him walk away from us, just because it suited me. I had to put their happiness and well-being first and it was better for them to have two parents living together than it was for us to split. Wasn't it?

Life went on, business as usual, for the next few years and things continued to decline between Nick and I. We no longer lived like husband and wife, we lived like roommates. We were completely disconnected from each other and lead completely separate lives; we didn't share the same bed, or at least not at the same time. In public, we played the part of happy family, but privately, when we were in each other's company, we ignored each other or fought. I had given up trying to find a way to connect with him and maintain a relationship and he simply never tried. The children were my sole responsibility; he worked and I budgeted the money, paid the bills, did the shopping, cooking, cleaning, took care of the kids and everything they needed. Doctors, dentists, activities, education; whatever the kids needed, I was the one and only person to get it done.

As we started to move out of the baby phase and into the we-have-three-potty-trained-children-who-sleep-through-the-night phase, Nick and I started trying to reclaim the friendship we once had. Even when the kids were with his mother on the weekends, our forced time alone together was still limited and extremely awkward.

Despite our lack of a "real" relationship (whatever that means), we thought having another baby was a good idea. After all, we no longer had our older three children home on weekends to distract us from the distance that had grown between us, so why not add one more to the dysfunctional family, right? On January 4, 2006, our youngest son, Jeffrey Tyler, was born. Nick and I were able to continue the façade that was our marriage just a little bit longer since I had this new little baby to consume all of my time.

And it almost worked.

But in the end, after 11 years of marriage, four children, the death of my mother, marriage counseling and trial separation, we filed for divorce on the grounds of "irretrievable breakdown of the marriage."

It was not a decision that was reached lightly, and in the end I suppose I was ultimately the one who made the call. Quite honestly, I had grown tired of the dishonesty in our marriage. I had grown tired of all of his late nights "working" and his lack of interest in sex… or sex with me at least! I was tired of the verbal abuse and the aggression that was becoming physical. Our relationship had become volatile. We were living a lie and it had gone on long enough. I finally found my backbone and realized that we were not modeling a healthy marriage for our children, and that they deserve better than this; better than the constant arguing and fighting between their parents, better than having a mother who is constantly stressed and upset, better than a father who is physically present but never emotionally present.

And when I made that realization, I swear I felt my mother's presence.

At a time when I needed her the most in my life, at a time when she was the only person who could have explained to me, because of her life experience, the difficult road that lay ahead of me as a divorced single mother, I felt this immense sense of calm wash over me as I sat on the bathroom floor balling my eyes out at the conscious decision I had just made, but had not verbalized to a single soul yet. I knew right then and there that, while difficult, I was making the right decision.

My choice to dissolve my marriage made me wonder: had I been too hard on my mother for not making it work with my father, for not fighting for her husband and trying to keep our family together? Now that I was a grown 30-something year old woman with children of my own and a failed marriage under my belt, I felt like I understood my mother a little bit better. Perhaps her decision not to fight for her marriage to my father is because she knew I would be better off without him. The only real clarity I gained is that when it comes to the dissolution of a family unit, there are no clear and easy answers. It's not black and white; there is plenty of gray area.

After spending my entire adult life belonging to Nick, this new found freedom and sense of independence I had as a divorcee was frightening and exciting all at the same time.

"We screw up, we lose our way. Even the best of us have our off days. Still we move forward." ~Meredith Grey, Grey's Anatomy

Freedom; it's a funny thing and most of us take it for granted. Until you've lived under the constant watch and demand of someone else, you really don't know what it's like to break free. It's scary as hell! It was scary when I was 16 and broke free of my mother's control and it was just as scary in my 30's, maybe even more so, breaking free of my marriage.

Freedom is a funny thing though, because those of us that aren't used to having so much of it tend to go a bit overboard.

In my short 30-something years, I had lived more than half of it under the absolute control of an abusive mother who cut me loose at 17, had a few shorts months to experience life on my own terms and then BAM! I ended up back in the control of another tumultuous relationship.

My divorce provided me with an overload of emotions, but funny enough, none of those feelings included regret. I had spent my entire marriage as a stay-at-home mom, per my ex-husband's wishes, and now as a divorced single mom with a household to support, four children to feed and a resume that had references that were twelve years old, I was screwed! Panic, stress and helplessness all set in pretty damn quick!

When I was able to wrap my head around things, I decided to start teaching art classes out of my basement. At the time, I was homeschooling my children (they had always been homeschooled) so I had plenty of connections in the homeschooling community. I began advertising in newsletters and online homeschool community lists, offering my "family art classes" one afternoon per week. The classes filled up so quickly that I soon had to add a second day of classes. For an entire year after my divorce, this was how I supported the family. But as winter drew near again, tuition from teaching alone wasn't going to pay for a winter's worth of heating bills here in New England. I racked my brain for other ideas, searched Craigslist for odd jobs and things I could do to earn money and still be at home with my kids.

After many failed attempts and bad interviews, I found something that sounded a little too good to be true. A small local newspaper was hiring freelance writers. The job didn't pay much, but there was the opportunity to write for various papers within their umbrella and make extra money. I sent the editor some writing samples and was immediately hired. My first story ended up on the front page! Finally, I felt like I might be able to handle this whole single mom business.

So where does the abuse of my new found freedom come in? Right now. Since I had figured out how to pay the bills and I had a pretty good handle on the kids, the visitation schedule and the divorce, I figured it was about time to start looking for a life of my own. After all, my kids were gone all weekend…every weekend. At first I felt guilty for even thinking about dating. Then I was scared because I had no idea how to meet people. Then worse, I started to remember what it was like growing up and my mother bringing various men into our lives. Then I worried about what my kids would think about me dating. Should I even tell them? When do I introduce them to someone I'm dating?

Yes, I overthink everything! What can I say? I'm a typical Type-A personality. Finally, one night, I bit the bullet and typed "online dating" into Google, you know, just to check it out. After hours of searching I decided to make a profile, but just a free one. I instantly had messages and winks and all kinds of flirty little online notifications. Wow! This could be fun! But it was so expensive! At $35 a month I just couldn't justify the cost, especially when I was working my ass off just to keep our heads barely above water. So I put it off for a while.

When I finally did take the plunge back into the dating world, I hid it from my kids. I wouldn't get ready for a date on Friday night until I knew they were gone to their dad's. I wouldn't have phone conversations with potential dates when they were home during the week and I kept all communications to text or online only. I figured that the best way to protect them was just not to involve them at all. Besides, I was newly divorced and wasn't looking for anything serious anyway, and 'serious' was the only way anyone was going to meet my kids so, no worries there, right?

Wrong! You see, my ex-husband moved directly across the street from me, into his parents' house, when we split up. So he still had that bit of control over me because he'd spy on me out the window and then tell the kids! I found myself trying to sneak around, leave my house quietly, and make sure no one ever came to my house. I felt like I was a cheating spouse or a sneaky teenager! Finally I decided that it was time to break it to the kids that I was dating.

Once I told them, and answered all of their questions, I think we all felt a little more comfortable. I know I did. They really didn't see it as a big deal. Phew! So I worried for nothing.

Now that the kids knew though, like a rebellious teenager I wanted to flex my new found freedom and do it while thumbing my nose at my ex. Mature, I know. This only infuriated him and caused our already disastrous divorce into pure torture. He began breaking into my house at all hours of the day and night. One night, he came in drunk and I had to lock myself in my bedroom and call the cops because he was trying to knock down my bedroom door. Another time he came over to get the kids, locked them outside, threw me against the wall and threatened to kill me. I saw my entire childhood flash before my eyes. I saw every shithead who ever put his hands on my mother, and I saw all of her feeble, yet courageous, attempts at fighting back. In that split second I found my backbone and decided that I was absolutely not going to let my kids grow up seeing their mother abused the way I did. I had had enough and I was finally putting my foot down. This time I went and got a restraining order.

My observations of my mother's 'relationships' while I was growing up, along with my own failed marriage, not to mention the abuse I suffered as a child, left me leery of men to say the very least. After about a year of dating various men, I had already had enough. I decided that I needed to work on me; that I needed to figure out who I was as a person, as a woman, before I could every truly be happy with anyone else. From that moment on, that's exactly where I spent my energy.

I had screwed up plenty, I had even lost my way for a bit, but now it was time to put one foot in front of the other and move forward with my life. The only problem was that I was still carrying around so much hate, resentment, anger and guilt from my childhood.

How could I move forward if I couldn't move past what was holding me back to begin with?

> *"Holding on to anger is like drinking poison and expecting the other person to die." ~Buddha*

I honestly don't think that one ever truly heals after the death of a parent, but I think this is especially true when the parent-child bond has been damaged. Not to discount the importance of the father-child bond or the mother-son bond, but there really exists no bond quite like that of mother and daughter. When you grow up without that bond, or you grow up with a dysfunctional mother-daughter relationship, I personally think it makes the grieving process that much harder once Mother dies.

It's been 15 years since I received that phone call from my mother; since I made that trek to Upstate New York, to her hospital room and since I told the nurse to abide by my mother's do not resuscitate order when she began gasping for her last painful breaths of air. It's been 15 very long, very trying, and often very emotional years. It's been 15 years of avoiding certain places because they remind me too much of her. It's been 15 years of guilt over carrying out her DNR order that night. It's been 15 years of regret over things left unsaid, and resentment over the fact that I will never get the closure that I so desperately wanted and still want to this day. And it's been 15 long years of nightmares and dreams involving her.

They say time heals all wounds. They lie. Time has certainly not healed the wounds that I have been left with. I often wonder if I will ever truly heal.

Some people say I should try therapy and perhaps they are right. The problem with therapy is that I'm not a particularly trusting person and I suck at communicating my feelings. Go figure, right? A kid who grew up never being hugged, never being told they were loved, never being told they were worth something, never being encouraged or built up in any way, has grown into an adult with attachment issues who has a problem with trust and communication. I don't think I need someone with a PhD in Psychology to tell me what the issue is. Anyone with an ounce of common sense in their head can figure out why I am the way I am and it's due mostly to a dysfunctional mother-daughter relationship.

So, how does one go about healing this relationship when one person dies?

I can't answer that for you. The secret that no one tells you, the secret that not one single book or therapist, friend or family member, clergymen or Tibetan monk can possibly answer for you is this: Only you can heal you.

I know what you're thinking, "This woman is out of her trees, and bat shit crazy!" I thought the same thing when my homeopath said it to me, but it's the truth. No one way is going to work for everyone. We are all different and we are all dealing with our own emotional wreckage from our dysfunctional mother-daughter relationships. There is no one-size-fits all method of dealing with the after-math of such a stormy relationship.

What has helped me feel a tiny bit closer to closure and just a little bit closer to healing has been self-discovery, communication and writing.

Taking the time to truly figure out who I am as a person, as a mother and as a woman has been essential to my mental health; really taking an honest look at my childhood and who I am today, how those events in my life shaped me into the person I am today. It's been a painful process because it requires me to remember and relive things that I honestly just want to erase from my memory, but I have found it to be necessary in beginning the recovery process.

Through self-discovery and really honest reflection, I came to the realization that my mother never really wanted me. If I look at her abusive childhood and compare it to mine, she used marriage as a way to escape an abusive, controlling mother, and I used college. She didn't have me because she wanted a child; she got pregnant by accident when she consummated her marriage to my father. She was stuck with me. Right out of the womb, my mother acted as though I owed her something for being born. This was proven over and over again as I went through life and she continually expressed her disappointment in me. I was born helpless and innocent. I was born with a right to some kind of safe environment and nurturing emotional atmosphere. But according to her actions over the years, I was more of a burden then I was a blessing. Perhaps my mother was not prepared for the responsibility and the overwhelming needs of a child? Perhaps she was lost in her own sea of self-doubt and perhaps her own value had never been established. But is that something that I should have to pay for? I think not, but it took me a long time to realize that.

It's taken me even longer to realize that while deep down my mother probably loved me in her own way, she also resented me. She resented all of the opportunity that lay ahead of me that she didn't have: graduating high school, going to prom, going off to college. She resented the life that she gave up by keeping me. She resented me for the choices she made because of me. And when she was so filled with resentment and anger towards me for all of the shit in her life that I really had no choice in or control over, she would lose control and take it out on me physically, verbally, emotionally or all three.

Throughout my life I have strived to be the exact opposite of my mother, but when it became clear that my marriage needed to end, I was afraid that my biggest fear had come true and that no matter how hard I tried, I was destined to become my mother. Looking back now, and through hours and even years of self-reflection, I know that this fear is unfounded. I am not my mother. I've had to say those words to myself thousands of time. I am NOT my mother. In moments of self-doubt, I repeat those words to myself like a mantra. I am NOT my mother.

Writing has always come easily for me as a way of self-expression. I have notebooks from my junior high and high school days filled with stories and poems that I wrote about various things going on in my life, emotions I was experiencing, or just plain old teenage angst. For me, writing is therapeutic. It's the only way I can truly express my feelings and emotions without judgment because there is no one involved except me and the paper, or these days the laptop screen. There is no one to interrupt me, no one to tell me that my feelings are unfounded or wrong. The laptop isn't going to tell me I'm crazy for feeling the way I feel or tell me to put on my big girl panties and just deal with it. When I'm writing I'm free to express myself in any words I choose and without judgment from anyone but myself. Sometimes my head gets so filled with memories and thoughts, or I'm so overcome with emotional baggage that if I sit down and just write all of the thoughts that are in my head and get it all off my chest, I feel a little bit better.

Writing letters to my mother has been a great exercise throughout the healing process. I know it sounds crazy because I'm essentially writing letters to someone who is dead, but trust me, it has worked wonders. The fact that my mother's death left me with so much unfinished business between the two of us meant that I was stuck with things that I felt I needed to say, but couldn't because how do you scream at a dead person? How do you have a conversation with an urn of ashes? I mean, I guess if you're the type of person who this works for then go for it! Who am I to judge if you want to yell and scream at a headstone or urn?! I won't judge. I'm writing letters to my dead mother.

The third component that I have found to be helpful is also the one that has been the hardest for me—communication. I openly admit that I absolutely suck at open, honest verbal communication, especially when feelings are involved. Sure, I can tell my kids that I love them and get all mushy and gushy with them, but they're my kids! When it comes to being vulnerable and openly expressing my own feelings, I lose all ability to form coherent sentences. My ex-husband can surely attest to my inability to share my feelings and emotions. I tend to keep everything bottled up inside me because that's how I was raised, that's how I'm programmed.

When you have trust issues and intimacy issues, it's difficult to be vulnerable with someone and communicate your thoughts and feelings. This has made relationships of most kinds, friendships as well as lovers, pretty freaking difficult, let me just tell you! When disagreements or arguments arise, I do one of two things: I get really nasty and lash out in very mean and hurtful ways because this was the example set for me growing up, or I completely shut down and withdraw. Neither is conducive to effective communication.

So how then have I been working through my grief with the use of communication as a tool? Well, I met someone who is pretty damn close to being the male version of me.

I was out Christmas shopping the Sunday after Black Friday in 2012 with Danielle, when she went racing into this sports store because they had a Stanley Cup replica in the window. The store owner, Sly, was very attentive and chatty, and very quick with the compliments, full of them really, but I paid very little attention to him or his compliments. I said very little, replying with an occasional, "Thank you," to one of his many compliments, with a quick glance up from checking emails on my phone. In all honesty, it took me a good 20 minutes, and Danielle nudging me when he wasn't looking, to realize that he was flirting with me.

Long story short—Danielle left with a $300 replica Stanley Cup and I left with his phone number. Within 24 hours we had plans to go out to dinner.

It was weird, I felt instantly comfortable with him. It was strange and scary all at the same time. I kept my guard up, but he was very intuitive. As the evening went on it became blatantly obvious that there was definite chemistry between us and it was more than just sexual chemistry. But neither one of us was looking for anything at all. I was just out of a string of relationships gone wrong and he was ending a 5-year relationship on a sour note. We just wanted to have fun that was it, that's what we agreed to. Neither of us was good at commitment, but we could both do fun. Fun is easy. Right?

Even reading that now and looking back it makes me laugh. The obvious connection between us, the chemistry, the intuitiveness, it all just intensified as we spent more time together. At one point I didn't have any contact with him for about 36 hours and, sensing something was wrong, he called to check on me. He was right. I was dealing with a childhood friend and his addiction and it was putting a huge strain on me, emotionally and physically. But how did this man, whom I barely knew, know that about me when the people closest to me barely realized?

Here we are a few years later and Sly can still sense when I'm uneasy, upset, withdrawing, stuck inside my head, stressed… no matter what it is that I'm feeling or going through, even when I don't say anything, he intuitively knows. He can read me very well; sometimes I hate this about him and other times I'm grateful.

Over the past couple of years I have been able to open up about so much to Sly and he simply listens. He doesn't judge, he rarely offers advice or suggestions, and when things get really emotional, he's there to wipe my tears and tell me everything is going to be OK. The flip side of this is that he's also there for all of the good as well as the bad.

I've never in my life had someone that I could completely, 100% be myself with, who accepts me 1000% just the way I am, perfectly imperfect. It's odd and awesome all at the same time. This person, whom I met in a mall store by chance, turns out to have so many things in common with me that we are literally almost male and female versions of each other. How does that happen? And how does he understand me so perfectly that sometimes, often times, he knows me better than I know myself? In him I have finally found the person, my person. He is the one and only person that I can show my soul to, be completely 100% vulnerable, and he accepts me without judgment.

But I went off on a mini tangent there, so back to the communication component of my healing process. Sly has been the person who has taught me how to better communicate my thoughts and feelings because of his acceptance of me and his patience with me. I know that no matter what is going on in my life, good or bad, he's got my back, and my heart. It's such a comforting feeling to know that, in my own limited capacity, I can communicate with someone on my terms about the good, bad and sometimes ugly inner workings of my heart and mind. I'm able to tell him things about myself that my ex-husband didn't even know, things Danielle doesn't even know!

Through communication with Sly, I am able to say things aloud that I haven't had the chance to say. I can tell him about the nightmares I have of the night my mother died and how I feel guilty, as if I murdered her. I can tell him of the dreams which include all of us having dinner with my mother, like a big happy TV family, and how devastated I am that it never happened and will never happen. I can talk to him about the mixed feelings I have about Mother's Day, or any other day when emotions are running high.

I'm the first person to admit that talking about emotions and feelings is no walk in the park, especially when those emotions are so raw and run so deep. I'm also going to admit that it is an essential part of the grieving and healing process.

The last thing to remember—you have to allow yourself to grieve before you can really begin to heal. Rabbi Dr. Earl Grollman once said, "Grief is not a disorder, a disease or a sign of weakness. It is an emotional, physical and spiritual necessity, the price you pay for love. The only cure for grief is to grieve."

"Healing doesn't mean the damage never existed. It means the damage no longer controls our lives." ~Akshay Dubey

It has taken me many years, 15 to be exact, to realize that healing and letting go of the pain doesn't negate the fact that it is all very real nor does it mean that it never happened. Allowing myself to heal simply means I am no longer allowing my past to control my present, or effect my future.

Yes, my mother was verbally, emotionally and physically abusive. Yes, my mother was emotionally unavailable. Yes, I experienced horrific trauma throughout my childhood that has had a lifelong psychological effect on me. Yes, I fantasize to this day about having the mother I saw on TV and in the homes of my friends. Yes, I loved my mother and hated her all at the same time. Yes, I am left with a tsunami of emotions to sort through still, 15 years later.

But I survived.

I spent a lot of years blaming my mother for the way I turned out, blaming her for my insecurities, intimacy and attachment issues, and maybe rightfully so.

But I survived.

The more I allow myself to work through the stages of grief and acceptance, the more I come to accept that while my childhood was anything but happy, without it I wouldn't be who I am, or where I am, today. The experiences I've had explain why I am the way I am, but they are not *who* I am.

I have a lot of my mother's traits; I'm a sarcastic, foul-mouthed, thick skinned Bostonian. I am fiercely independent, determined, and don't take no for an answer. I am stubborn, passionate (although some might say hot-headed), and don't take shit from anybody. I say whatever pops into my head and that may sound rude to some, but you know where you stand with me because I'm honest; I don't sugar coat anything for anyone.

I also have a lot of traits my mother didn't; I'm compassionate and affectionate. I tell and show my kids every day that I love them. I don't abuse my children in any way, shape or form. I know that discipline doesn't have to mean parenting with an iron fist. I build my children up, encourage them to be and do anything they set their mind or heart to, the sky's the limit!

Healing for me has meant growing up and growing wiser. I learned that not only did I need to grieve the loss of my mother and the relationship I never had with her, but I also needed to grieve the loss of my childhood. I had to grieve what I went through as a little girl; grieve that I didn't have, and would never have, the loving mother I wanted.

Since my mother was an addict, part of my grieving and healing process has taken part with groups such as Al-anon and nar-anon. These groups are for the families of the addict and/or alcoholic. I never really bought into the entire program, mostly because I don't believe in God, but also because I don't really like the whole group therapy session mentality. However, the group's motto is "Take what you like, and leave the rest," and there are some quotes and thoughts that I have found helpful:

- *"You didn't cause it, you can't control it and you can't cure it."*
- *"You must learn a new way to think before you can master a new way to be."*

- "If you don't like being a doormat, then get off the floor."
- "It is what it is."

It is what it is. That pretty much sums up my entire dysfunctional relationship with my mother. Sure I could spend the rest of my life locked in this cycle of grief, resentment, anger, and desire for closure that I will never have, but why? It won't change anything; it is what it is. The past is the past, and you can't change it, but you can learn from it.

Over the past 15 years I've struggled with depression, grief, guilt, anxiety; I've been tormented by nightmares and haunted by memories.

But I survived.

Made in the USA
Middletown, DE
02 February 2015